Opening The Windows Of Your Soul

by

MADISON KING

Young Faces Smiling

Young Faces Smiling Publishing Company

455 Tarrytown Road,

White Plains, New York 10607

Book Cover Designed by: Pixel Studio
Book Layout Designed by: Lisa Smiph
Authors: Madison King and A. McClarty
Editors: A. McClarty and Copeland
All photos courtesy of the author, Young Faces Smiling
Printed in the United States of America

Names: King, Madison, McClarty, A. – Authors
Title: Opening The Windows of Your Soul
Description: New York: NYC Public School – Student and Poetry
Subjects: LCSH: King, Madison (Student)
McClarty, A. and Young, Dr. Eloise L – Founders of Young Faces Smiling

LCCN List

1. NYCDOE   2. Non-Profit   3. Education Enrichment Program

4. Student   5. Poetry   6. Becoming an Author

ISBN: 978-1-957978-00-0

Table of Contents

Dedication

Ebony King

My Mother

Who birthed me and passed down all her amazing reading and
writing skills.

Thanks Mom!

Acknowledgements

I would like to express my gratitude to "The Man Above" who supported me and trusted my process when no one else did.

I am also extremely grateful for my third-grade teacher, Ms. Ferraro, who saw the talent in me when I was too shy to embrace it.

I would also like to acknowledge my teacher Ms. Myrie who I feel invested in me and contributed to the development of my writing, and the perspective in which I see writing and literature in.

Finally, but never last, I am so grateful for my principal Mrs. S. Nicholas for giving me the opportunity to become an author. Thank you Ms. Copeland and Ms. McClarty (the two ladies of Delta Sigma Theta Sorority, Inc) for making sure this moment happen. Thank you to Ms. Gaddy.

Young Faces Smiling has given me the chance to become a published author. I am so immensely thankful for making one of my biggest dreams become true.

THE SCHOOL BY THE SEA ~ P.S./M.S. 43Q
MISSION STATEMENT:

The School by the Sea ~ P.S./M.S. 43Q is a 3K-8 college
and career preparatory public school located in the
Far Rockaway community of Queens, New York.

Our goal is to develop children into leaders by providing
them with a quality education that will prepare them for
success in high school, college and beyond.

The School by the Sea ~ P.S./M.S. 43Q will serve to meet
the individual needs of our children academically and
socially. Our school will provide students with a rigorous
education as well as meaningful collegiate and
professional connections.

As a result, children will grow with the personal
motivation necessary to succeed and inevitably develop
into well-rounded, productive citizens.

ROBOT

Feelings

Thoughts, emotions and pain
Flood me like a tsunami

What Shall I do?

Shall I dig a hole
So deep where the pains lives
And bury the burdens
I call feelings

Are my feeling beating me
In this war I call life?

Am I losing?

Why is it so hard to have apathy?
I am no robot
Having apathy makes me weak

Have no feelings makes me weak and powerless,
And I know that does
But do I seek power?
Not entirely

I seek inner peace
Wisdom and Serenity

I know its within me
But how do I activate it?
How do I withstand urge to go numb and in Robot mode

And just not feel

The motivation will come from my father up above
And from the infinite love that runs for myself

Feelings are human
And I am Just of the sort

SAY THEIR NAMES

George Floyd a victim of racism at hand
We march for the BLM protest to stand
Cries and pleads and rears shed

Get off his neck

No luck

The day he left, woke people up
The blind could see the everyday problems

The people in frustration, showed consideration
The people in disbelief said it was a
Misunderstood situation?

Believe the unbelievable
Have some faith
Without video y'all wouldn't believe his fate

He left us all blue and it's too sad to be true
When we are supposed to draw inside the lines
We pray for our lives scared to go outside
Scared to realize that our lives are taken without
any consideration or time.

Reunited with his mother, his love for her is true
His soul is in a better place, his spirit runs free
Like a dog, unleased at a dog park
When he left he set a boundary, a tolerance,

Fake realities, where all is equal
Lethal Murders
Like a never-ending movie with brutal sequels

He just wanted some acceptance,
Like the rest of them who wait in heaven
We can't get back the lives we lost
So, we will gain more by equality and change for all

Say Their Names

George Floyd
Daunte Wright
Breonna Taylor
Tamir Rice
India Kager
Darius Robinson
Janet Willison
Emmet Till

CHATTER

you were wilted
you were almost dead
struggling to stand up on your own

I watered you
Gave you sun
Made you, your own flower

you were crippled and used me like a cane
you sucked me dry, and used me to keep yourself sane
you tricked me and I fell right into your trap
you fed me all your manipulative sap

Why did you pick me?
Why me?
An innocent bystander that stumbled into your life
you used me
stabbed me in the heart with a knife

Right in front of me
you stabbed me in front of my two eyes
I never felt the pain till I saw it with my eyes

I sacrificed me, for your life
In the end it didn't matter
your promises for being best friends forever
was just chatter

I gave to you all I could give
poured my heart and soul into you

You were a lesson, MY lesson to learn
My test

If our friendship were to fall
Would I go up into flames and burn?

WAKE UP

Imagine
you're comfy in this seat
you're in your safe place
you're with the right people

Seizing the minutes of everyday
Blooming like a flower
Building your life, Like a tall, tall tower

And Boom
One day all that stuff that you know,
That you love
That seat that was once comfy gets pulled from
beneath you

Life is a harsh reality
Life is also filled with amazing opportunities
But life is unpredictable

It's like a water slide with an indefinite amount of
twist and turns
Life doesn't care: it has no concerns
There is no such thing as comfortable
Because reality

Simply exists

WHO AM I, REALLY?

Top of the class
Being home at curfew
Listening to your mom
Never bending the rules

Reading instead of drinking
Google classroom instead of drugs
Thinking about your future instead of staying out late
Clean mouth instead of a dirty one

That's my life…..

In most people's eyes that's good

But that other side of me
That other side of me curious
To do stuff I would never even imagine
Just to fit the image of "cool"

This isn't my image of cool
My mind put people who live that lifestyle
On a pedestal and categorized me boring
Yet part of me wants to try it out
Part of me wants to ditch who I am

Im boring but safe
Am I living?
I'm alive but am I living
Am I where I'm supposed to be at this age?
Doing what I'm supposed to do?
I'm puzzled

My good trouble-free life is me

And they say be authentic

CHANGE

Change, what is change?
No, what exactly is change?
It's funny because when you think of change
you think of something or someone that is going
to be different

You think of an evolved soul
You think of something new

People make past and synonym
No one lets you escape
Nor forget who you once were
Really past and change are two different things

Hypocrites
People preach for change but constantly remind you
of who you once were.

Change

When you allow the lightness to shine in on your
own ways

Believe it or not but a thug, thief or robber can be in
the somebody as a doctor or lawyer

No, I get it your past is always attached
Like a dog, with its tail

A Tree, the leaves of a tree were once orange and
multi colored
But should we shame the tree for turning green
Should we remind the tree of the colors, it shed
off, constantly?

The difficult part is change is trust
Sometimes you dig, yourself so deep in
That change is of the essence
Your Misjudged and sometimes, it's too late
Sometimes you work so hard......

But, the real reality is that your slate sometimes
Can't be clean.

TO BE BRAVE

Brave to do precarious things that put your
dignity at risk
Bravery, real bravery is when nerves and
Anxiety is creeping up your spine

like you're getting the chills

Brave
When your struggling to walk because your legs
are overcome by shaking

When your heart feels like it's going to burst
in your chest
When your mind is filled with anxiety
and thoughts and doubts of the outcome

But,

Bravery is also when you dig your nerves a grave
And bury them alive
To be brave is to choose not to be embarrassed

To be brave is to visualize the outcome and go
face first into danger
Bravery is not to be held back by chains
But to break free and seize opportunities

Bravery is a bird

A bird that's facing flying or falling
Out its nest when firstly being bought in this world

Bravery is in all of us

It's up to us whether we let that be held back by
fear

MY INNER MONSTERS

Were you ever afraid of the dark?
When the light switched off
Were you afraid of what you couldn't see

Why?

Why? Why were you so afraid?

Or maybe you still are

Maybe you're still afraid of the monsters
Under the beds or in the closets
Or in your head
Maybe you hate the dark
They say what you can't see can't hurt you

But deep down you question that statement
Wait why are you so afraid

Some People love the dark
They love that it's a blanket to hide their
insecurities under
They make friends with the monsters
under the bed
And the inner voices in their heads

They see no harm in not seeing
They thrive when everything is hidden
When what you hate about yourself is
pushed under the rug, where others can't see it

When it's dark, silence usually follows

Silence is when the voices come back
When you can hear
or feel guilty
for these people being in the dark isn't a shield
it's a ...
Microphone, thoughts on a loudspeaker
The demons in your head come back and
take over
And drown you with your deepest insecurities
So, I guess I'm asking which one are you?

GREEN

The power of a dollar
Why does this piece of paper have so much value?

Would you kill a friend and leave your kids
For a dollar?

This dollar got you wrapped around its finger
Like a tight collar

What does a few couple of bills buy you?
Happiness?

It's like this money got you stuck on a lead
Is this what you really need.

Will you let a couple of bills change your life,
your money could be gone in a roll of a dice

Once this money runs out you're on thin ice.
you become infested with greed like a head of lice

Why does this piece of paper have so much value?

WINDOWS OF YOUR SOUL

You think you know someone like the back of your
Hand
Until your friendship starts sinking like quicksand

Expeditiously, Rapidly fast

It's hard to think, that person was in them
That dark maliciously evil twin of there's
It's funny how they can flip personalities
Like you flip a coin

I was blind

But I wasn't

Their evil twin peaked out sometimes

I knew it, I knew it and I stayed

They showed me their real colors
And opened the windows of their soul
Still in my head I painted them out to be beautiful

Why was I pretending to be blind for so long?

I failed me

I'm sorry

I failed me.

SLOW DOWN

Take a minute
look at the leaves and how they flow
The spine of the tree's
The ombre color leaves

The new blooming flower buds
Tree branches drape over creating shade
The way the wind flows and brushes your face

Breathe because you get the chance to
look at the birds building their nest so peacefully
look now the birds fly and soar, they feel so free

Take a minute, to observe the peaceful nature
because you can
I bet you've wanted to be a bird at least once
No I'm sorry not a physical bird
But to have the feeling of a bird

To be free to have passage wherever you want
To run away
Or should I say fly away
To have nothing to look back for with each step

Or would you want to feel like a star
Something with many definite purposes
Or did you wish you was ocean that just
went with the flow.

No?

Maybe a pirate who loves and trust his ship
so much that he let's the ocean steer his vessel

Maybe you want to be a lion
King of the Jungle
Breathe not because others don't get to
But because you do

BLM

Why did y'all get to choose
Who's life was desirable
Why did y'all get to separate an offspring from it's
Mother

Whipped us until we were lifeless
And sold my body like you were a broker
Why was my kinky hair so hated?

Why did our existence bother you?

Why were my ancestors getting lynched from trees
like we were a clothing article
Why do you presume me uneducated, destitute and
ugly

Because of my skin color
Because of my rich brown and black roots
that run throughout my soul

Why do you have this deep branch of supremacy
growing in you
people died
My people died

My people died from your so called "Justice Servers"
your police

So, I say **Black Lives Matter** with all my
heart
with all my veins
And life I have in my body

We were all placed under the same moon
As equals
It's about time y'all start acting like it

DIGGING DEEPER INTO VENGEANCE

They always say two wrongs don't make a right

Fight or Flight
The night way is always flight
Always take the high road

Be the bigger person

But Why?
Why should I be the bigger person?
Why should I excuse their faults and let
my conscience worsen?
Why should I walk away?

Why shouldn't I wrong the person that did me wrong
They tell me that walking along is strength and
power

But sometimes I fight the urge to power back
To retaliate to get my revenge

Like a dog on a lease
I fight back every temptation in my body to not
turn to darkness

Revenge is grudge holding
Grudge holding leaves you stuck
Being stuck makes you bitter

While it's so easy to give into temptation

I rather walk away then be bitter.

TURNING YOUR EYES INSIDE

Being self-assured, being self-aware
Knowing you're self inside and out
Seeing all your faults and loving it because you're you
That's confidence

Confidence is acceptance and love
Confidence is turning your eyes inside and seeing
your imperfections first hand.
And saying "I'm Perfect"
It's the best feeling in the world
No, it's not only a feeling it's a mentality

You have to think it before you are "it"
Confidence is a force field to insecurity
Confidence is internal

But when you have to shout your worth to other people
You're really trying to get yourself to listen
To believe it
Insecurities hide behind cockiness, don't confuse
the two.

If you know your worth
Others will think of you very highly
And perceive you highly

BAITED

A costume and makeup is a really good disguise
If we take it all off it's really just a lie

A Clown

The same clown that stabbed you in the back
had you running back.
With your name attached to the knife he held
So smugly.

Who's really the clown here?
The person that showed their true colors?
Or the person who's still here?

Even though they reveal their true colors,
Makeup like a clown you still constantly decide to
stay around

Congrats you made it out the circus,
You hear his voice lurking within.
The rhythm of the beat that he sang, we thought
you had overcome,
he flipped the script I made a conflict

He sold you in with the biggest grin
You revealed your trips and tricks

I believed in you but you gave back in

Ride or die

You rode with the leader, turned down the block

Now your in a one seater

Playing a game of twister
Did he twister your mind?

Did he twist your mind?

Or did you fall back in the same crime.

HERO AND VILLAINS

Heroes are great
They save the day
When they lay their heads down at night
Their hearts are bright
shining with good intention

They're destined to win

Their pictures are painted already

Happy endings

They always win

But what if villains won just this once?

Villains are villains because of their good
share of bad people

Their happiness always gets stripped

Villains aren't born they're made
They seek vengeance against people that
did them wrong

We've all had a villain's mentality before

Villains are more realistic
Not everyone thinks good all the time
Villains are people who have been wronged
So the next time you see a "bad guy"
Ask yourself
What made them so bad?
What made them want revenge
What made them wicked?
What did someone do to send them on their
dark path?

Then make your judgment

Are they a villain or deeply in sorrow?

About The Author

MADISON KING

Hello I am MADISON KING. I was born and raised in New York City. I was born in the month of June.

I have a passion for all things creative. My mind is an imaginative construction site constantly building new ideas and generating new ways to express myself. My thinking itself is art. I favor the fiction genre for reading and writing. I wrote this book of poetry not only to inspire people, but for people to relate to me.

Although I love writing, I also have a passion for fashion and I am thinking of going into the medical field later on in my life. Two pieces of advice I have for my readers or even my writers out there is to be AUTHENTIC. No one know you like you and no one has the same experiences as you. So, use that as an advantage. Also do not limit your mind. Sometimes a plan is like a fork in the road, choose a road and do not force your mind in a box.

About The Principal

PRINCIPAL
SIMONE A. NICHOLAS

A native of Brooklyn, New York and the granddaughter of Caribbean immigrants from Guyana, St. Vincent, and Grenada, West Indies, Simone A. Nicholas was raised in a village where the core values of education, social action and service to the community were grounded. Principal Nicholas received her Bachelor's Degree in Sociology and African-American Studies at Dartmouth College, two Master's Degrees in Education, and Administration/Supervision from C.U.N.Y. Brooklyn College, and will receive her Educational Doctorate from Manhattanville College in 2023.

Prior to beginning her educational career, Principal Nicholas worked in the legal profession where she assisted in winning multi-million dollar cases in wrongful death, malpractice and personal injury lawsuits. She began her teaching career in 1996 at a Middle School in Bedford Stuyvesant, Brooklyn and has since held various school and Central based roles across all five boroughs within the New York City Department of Education.

Principal Nicholas is the first Female and first African American Female Principal of The School by the Sea ~ P.S./M.S. 43Q located in Far Rockaway, Queens New York. A Social Justice & Equity Champion for Children, she has expanded instructional rigor, affected school climate, doubled student proficiency scores and removed the school from New York State's failing school list to place the school back in Good Standing. Continuing the mission to foster a culture of excellence, equity and determined to provide access at all levels for her children, families and community, Principal Nicholas ensures students participate in all-expense paid HBCU tours and offers exemplary Restorative Justice and STEAM extra-curricular programs. Principal Nicholas has been the recipient of multiple local, state and federal academic and social emotional learning grants and has increased community engagement through workshops that promote instructional and social-emotional strategies to impact student success. In addition, the school has expanded adult learning programs such as financial literacy awareness, GED classes, access to various community agencies to provide on the spot jobs with training, and has worked with advocates and community-based organizations to ensure the school is a flagship food and health hub for the community. Principal Nicholas also sits on various local and Citywide committees such as the Chancellor's Principal Advisory Cabinet, New York State Senatorial 10th District Education Committee; NYC My Sisters' Keeper Collaborative; and Community School District 27 CR-SE/Black History Month Program Committee. Principal Nicholas has also humbly accepted Proclamations and Awards from local, state and national legislators and organizations for her mentorship and advocacy within the Far Rockaway community.

With over 35 years of commitment to public service and leadership, Principal Nicholas is a Legacy Life member and President of the National Council of Negro Women, Inc., Long Island Cross County Section and a member of the National Coalition of 100 Black Women, Long Island Chapter. Principal Nicholas also serves as a Dartmouth College Ambassador Interviewer who advocates for diversity and equity practices to ensure admissions for students of African descent remains a priority. Lastly, Principal Nicholas is a founding member of "Black Ed-fluencers United (BE-U)" and "The Off School Grounds (OSG)" educational coalitions created to provide a platform for leaders to network and share best practices for growth and development, while advocating for the success and equity in education for underserved communities with a focus on Black and Brown children and families.

Principal Nicholas is a member of Christian Cultural Center and currently resides in Baldwin, New York with her loving husband and their blended family of 4 awesome young adults.

About The Founders

Ms. A. McClarty

Ms. McClarty is a permanent certified New York State teacher for grades pre-K through 6 and has taught in Albany and NYC public schools since 1993. She also holds certification in Administration/Supervision and Educational Leadership. Since that time, she has been involved in a number of entrepreneurial endeavors.

Ms. McClarty is co-founder of Young Faces Smiling. Following her experience as a teacher and administrator in Albany and NYC Board of Education, she launched the vision. Ms. McClarty joined forces with her mentor, Dr. Young, to create Young Faces Smiling where real life opportunities are used to motivate and educate students on at the outskirts of society and in need of a drastic intervention.

Ms. McClarty took her 1999 fifth-grade students through a series of classroom exercises in which she introduced them to the concept of reading current event articles and writing pen-pal letters to celebrities, entrepreneurs and public figures.

These letters included concerns, questions and comments about the article. This *Reality Teaching* technique inspired her to broaden her horizons and became the basis of her entrepreneurial venture.

Ms. McClarty is currently working on her Doctoral Degree in Education Leadership.

DR. ELOISE L. YOUNG

D r. Eloise L. Young had a vision to help those in need and once the opportunity presented itself, she was unhesitant in establishing this organization. Dr. Young has served as Chaplain of Westchester County, which involved counseling residents of various County institutions located in Valhalla namely, the Department of Corrections, the Psychiatric Institute, the Geriatric Center and the Westchester Medical Center for over thirty years. Working alongside the Social Services Department, Dr. Young helped to promote a Sesame Street Program which allowed children of inmates to be transported to the facility once a month to spend time with their mothers.

A businesswoman in her own right, Dr. Young owned and operated her church, Religious Hut, the first Christian Bookstore in the town of Greenburgh. Dr. Young's impact has been far reaching and a dissertation expounding her religious beliefs and philosophy has been placed in the Law Library at Harvard University. Dr. Young received an honorary doctorate. Dr. Young returned to school and graduated from The College of New Rochelle at the age of 71. In the heart of Dr. Young are America's youth and the people at large.

Young Faces Smiling

YOUNG FACES SMILING is a 501©(3) non-profit founded by Dr. Eloise L. Young and Ms. A. McClarty in 2005. The organization primary objective is to motivate, inspire and encourage students.

Our Mission: Young Faces Smiling is an innovative educational enrichment program that connects students to celebrities and their career experiences.

Our Vision: Young Faces Smiling primary goal is to empower young people in school and in the community. YFS is an in-class literacy-based program that utilize pop culture as a catalyst to effect positive academic change. Through a partially student-directed curriculum a multiplicity of methods and approaches will be utilized to teach students. YFS will focus on the real history of celebrities, entrepreneurs, and public figures that provide real-life examples that transforms into an educational enrichment program.

Our Enrichment Program: Young Faces Smiling
Informed by the current research, YFS addresses two of the soft skills, tenacity and persistence to address student academic performance. Students identify with celebrities, entrepreneurs and public figures that they would like to meet; they will read current articles, which highlight biographical information, secrets to their success, and pitfalls to avoid; finally, they write letters grounded in one or two facts culled from the article read. YFS curriculum is not limited to letter writing, which is entirely structured on factual information but other subject areas are used during the program. YFS will deliver on their promises to connect students with them. Sometimes it only takes one person to motivate and change the life of another and students are destined to have a memorable lifetime experience with them.

Young Faces Smiling thrives on the kindness of celebrities, entrepreneurs and public figures to enrich the professional learning experience of students, thus creating visionaries, instilling hope and revitalizing student potential. YFS lessons will focus on the 'Real History' of celebrities, entrepreneurs and public figures that provide real-life examples and academic problems. YFS also use pop culture as a hook, integrating reading, writing, social studies, science, math, and technology. YFS assist in the transformation of the students and ensure them with confidence in themselves and competency in their academics. YFS expose students to career pathways provided through interviews, job shadowing and interactions with the celebrity involved.

Young Faces Smiling is a unique partnership and collaboration between celebrities and professional industry that have a keen focus to assist in improving the educational experience and outcomes of at-risk youth. It is our intent to help reverse the rising rates of school dropouts, joblessness, incarceration among youth, and to increase their representation in the pipeline to higher education and professional endeavors.

Testimonial

- "The most important ingredient in success is getting a good education and developing the right habits. All of the students are at the time when they can do both." – Warren Buffett, CEO/ Founder of Berkshire Hathaway, Inc.

Young Faces Smiling is an educational enrichment program for all students, irrespective of color, class or creed.

Social Media

Follow Young Faces Smiling on YouTube, Facebook, Twitter, Instagram, Clubhouse and more.

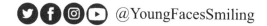 @YoungFacesSmiling

*** Go to our YouTube page to see several celebrity interviews. www.youngfacessmiling.org

Don't Forget to Order OUR INSPIRING BOOKS at YFS Store – www.youngfacessmiling.store